T0095160

Twice In Love

AMIN DURANT

Order this book online at www.trafford.com
or email orders@trafford.com

Most Trafford titles are also available at major online book retailers.

Edited by Artelu Consultants
Box 178, Road Town
Tortola, British Virgin Islands

Email: rswain@email.com or avril_25@hotmail.com

Please send or refer all feedback and/or requests for additional information to:

New Artist Production}
P.O. Box 2197
Road Town, Tortola
British Virgin Islands

Tel: 284 545 6887
Or
Email: twiceinlove@hotmail.com

Printed in the United States of America.

ISBN: 978-1-4269-5779-6 (sc)
ISBN: 978-1-4269-5780-2 (hc)
ISBN: 978-1-4269-5781-9 (e)

Library of Congress Control Number: 2011902196

Trafford rev. 03/08/2011

 www.trafford.com

North America & international
toll-free: 1 888 232 4444 (USA & Canada)
phone: 250 383 6864 ♦ fax: 812 355 4082

A MESSAGE FROM THE AUTHOR

It is always sensible to learn from the experiences and problems of others. Many of us are trying to get the best we can get out of our love relationships or sexual experiences and the unlucky ones are only too aware that these aspects of their lives are unfulfilling.

We must learn to discover ourselves so that we can better understand our partners. That's the only way dysfunctional relationships can improve.

I hope this book will bring you food for thought.

Ideally, sex should be an intrical part of the covenant of matrimony. In reality, sex is often used solely as a source for pleasure and escape from the hassles of life.

I leave this thought with you…Always remember that the future belongs to those who take care of themselves in the present.

CHAPTER ONE

It was a beautiful summer's day back in August. A warm tropical breeze was blowing through the Sir Francis Drake Channel. The sky was clear. The water was as still as a mirror. In fact, the weather was so good, Max decided to spend the day on the beach with his family.

Together, he and his wife loaded the family's van with light snacks and drove into town. There they caught the ferry over to Virgin Gorda and once they arrived, they rented a jeep and headed to the Baths…one of the best swimming sites in the British Virgin Islands.

The afternoon seemed to melt away, as Max took the time to really enjoy the closeness of his family. He loved his wife, Kara and daughters dearly. Even though he was currently out of work and had financial pressures, he was thoroughly enjoying himself.

Max and his family settled in a semi-private part of the beach and after a while, he took out his trusted camera and began to take pictures of the happy group, who were enjoying themselves, splashing in the warm, crystal clear water. He wanted to ensure that the gorgeous day would be immortalized forever!

After shooting a few rolls, he took a rest on a beach chair, while the wife and kids slipped into the warm seawater to bathe.

The cool breeze was beginning to gently rock him to sleep, when a voice interrupted his tranquility. Max opened his eyes to see a stranger standing over him with a broad smile on his face.

"I've been observing how well you handle yourself with that camera" said the stranger, who later introduced himself as Thomas.

"Thanks man. I'm Max", replied Max, "but I must confess …it's my job…I'm a professional photographer, my specialty is shooting models and you must admit…I have three beautiful models to work with" Max took every opportunity to boast about Kara and the girls.

"I see", said Thomas, "So have you had any exciting work recently?"

"Well things are really kind of slow right now. I'm just taking it one day at a time", Max confessed to him.

"You have a lovely family, Max." Thomas said, attempting to change the subject, sensing that he had hit a nerve. Then, out of nowhere, he asked, "So what would your wife think about relocating?"

Max was a little taken back, but he somehow managed to muster a reply, "Well, I really never thought about it, but it might be a good idea. Anyway, enough about me! Tell me about yourself, Thomas".

That was just what he wanted. This man, practically a total stranger, jumped at the opportunity to fill him in on the details of his life.

"I'm married, with three kids; two boys and one girl, but I'm in the midst of a divorce. My wife decided that after fourteen years together, she doesn't want to be married to me anymore," explained Thomas.

Then without stopping for Max to respond, he went on, "She said that she's spent too much of her time taking care of me and the kids and that she needs some time to spread her wings and explore life. She figures she can't do that being married to me", Thomas further explained; his voice filled with emotion.

"sorry about that, man!" Max said, in his best attempt at being empathic, trying to make Thomas feel a little better.

"That's ok. I think I have adjusted pretty well. I have my own advertising business in Trinidad. It's doing well and I'm kept very busy," he went on to say, his voice beginning to return to normalcy.

"Right now we're looking for an experienced professional photographer and my gut feeling is, you fit that description! So what do you say? Are you interested in the job or not?" Thomas inquired, causing Max to gasp in surprise.

"Whoa...you sure don't waste time at all," replied Max, trying to keep focused on reality.

"I'm a businessman Max, and in business, time is money! Exclaimed Thomas, almost in an aggravated manner.

"So let me ask you, Thomas...if I do decide to take this job, it would mean I have to move to Trinidad, right?" Max inquired. The thought of the sudden incredible opportunity began to sink in.

"Precisely, Max!" Thomas responded, sensing that he had gained Max's interest.

"Well, if that's the case. I would definitely have to talk this over with the wife and kids", Max told him, being as frank as he could be.

"I have no problem with that…but don't take too long making up your mind. Remember time is money! After you've discussed it with your family and decided what you want to do, give me a call. Here's my card" Thomas replied, while he slipped his business card into Max's hand. Thomas then shook Max's hand and walked away just as suddenly as he had approached him, only moments earlier.

On the ferry back to Tortola, Max approached Kara with the offer that Thomas had made to him about the job in Trinidad.

"Kara…we need to talk, honey," Max told her.

"Is something wrong, baby?" she asked, her voice sounding so sweet and caring.

"Well yes and no, honey. Remember that guy I was talking to on the beach today?" he questioned.

"How can I possibly forget Thomas. You spent a great deal of what was supposed to be our time together, talking with him," she said, her voice sounding a bit tensed.

'he offered me a job, Kara…in fact, a very good job!" Max bragged.

"That's wonderful Max! when do you start?" she asked enthusiastically.

"That's the problem honey. The job is in Trinidad," he explained.

Right away, without any hesitation, whatsoever, Kara exploded, "Max! My mom's here…my dad's here. All of our friends are here. I don't want to…no, I won't move! Tell that man you can't accept the job!"

"But honey, we need the money. I was thinking that maybe I could go for a while…like three months or so and see how it goes." Max said, trying to console and calm her.

"Anyway we take it Kara, I still have to come back to you and the kids. So how about it?" he asked, knowing fully well that he was treading on thin ice.

"Max, I don't think I can handle that. What if it takes you more than three months?" she asked.

"Baby, if you don't want me to go, I won't go…but when you think about it, it would probably be for the best.

"Things are very slow here. It's been so for the past few months. Our finances are dwindling and sooner or later there won't be any money left for me to support you and the girls. So you see, honey, we need this job to stay afloat", Max coached her, in his attempt to make her see reality from his perspective.

"Oh, ok Max…you've made your point…but, promise me…only for three months!" she said, finally beginning to see where he was coming from.

"Thanks honey! I love you!" he replied, holding her gently in his arms.

three weeks later, Max boarded the plane. He was on his way to the land of steel band, limbo and calypso!

And so started Max's adventure!

However, when he arrived in Trinidad, he found it to be very different from what he had expected. Life there moved at a lot faster pace than he was accustomed to. He felt out of place. He had no friends; no one he could trust.

But...over the following weeks, as he grew familiar with this new environment, things began to gradually change. Thomas made sure of that!

Max was introduced to Thomas' inner circle of friends, his business acquaintances and a seemingly endless supply of gorgeous women. Soon after, he had himself totally convinced that he could get used to this new lifestyle.

CHAPTER TWO

Wanting to make a good impression, Max made sure he got to Thomas' agency very early each day.

"Max, I see that you are one of the early birds…but I want you to know that I am not easily impressed," said Thomas, amusingly, yet, in his own business-like way.

"Good morning Thomas" replied Max. At that point, he didn't know if Thomas was only kidding or if he was just very strict.

And…before Max could bring himself to say anything else, remotely intelligent, Thomas rambled on, "This is Rose, your secretary. She is going to show you around the office, so you'll be comfortable in our little neck of the woods!"

Max nodded at the plump, slightly older woman, who would be his assistant for the next three months.

"I'll check on you later, after you've settled in, "Thomas told him.

"Thanks again for everything" Max replied, finally getting a word in.

"No problem man" was Thomas' reply, before he shot off to take care of business as usual.

As Thomas was safely out of sight, Rose immediately took the opportunity to get acquainted with her new boss.

"Tell me Max…what do you think about our island so far" Rose asked, with her sweet "*Trini*" accent.

"Well, I haven't seen much of it, but I must say that I am very much impressed with what I have seen," he answered.

"Good for you! I hope you won't be disappointed!" she said. A smile began to form on her rosy cheeks as she spoke.

"No, I don't think I would be. After all…I'm a man who likes adventures, so I'm pretty sure I'll find more than enough things while I'm here to keep me busy," Max told her…a trace of the Caribbean Man in him beginning to show itself.

"I hope so, but just in case you get bored, give me a call and I'll definitely find something for you to keep busy!" she offered, almost in a sultry, yet innocently sweet manner.

"Thanks, Rose" her replied, not sure where the conversation was heading.

"That's what I am her for, Max…to make sure that you're comfortable and that all of your needs are taken care of," she explained.

"All of my needs?" he asked jokingly.

"Well, not all, but most of them" she quickly replied, sensing that perhaps Max had something devious in mind.

"Just kidding, Rose!" he replied. He quickly tried to bring the conversation back to some form of professionalism.

I'm glad you have a sense of humor. Most bosses these days don't even know how to laugh, much less, have a sense of humor…but I can see that you're different. I hope you won't change with time!" she said.

"I promise you, Rose…I won't" Max assured her.

"You promise?" she asked softly.

"You have my word, Rose!" he assured her.

A few days later, Thomas checked in on Max to see how he was adjusting to the job. It wasn't that he did not trust Max. He certainly had no doubts about his ability. Thomas just wanted to make sure everything was going all right. He had major plans for Max that he hadn't discussed with anyone.

"So Max…how is the new office? I trust everything is to your liking," Thomas asked, when he popped his head into Max's office.

I'm comfortable. I must say I have no complains," replied Max.

"That's good Max. As long as you're happy, I'm happy," he explained…and in the same breath, he turned to Rose and asked her, "Did you give Max his assignment for today?"

Rose answered "Not yet, Sir. I was waiting for John. Sorry Sir, I did not think…"

"That's the problem with you people! You don't think! It looks like I have to do all of the thinking around here!" Thomas shouted, before she could finish. The he turned around abruptly and stormed out of the door, down the corridor and into one of the outer offices.

Max felt so bad for her, all he could do was apologize to the poor lady, "I am awfully sorry about that, Rose," he consoled her.

"That's ok…I'm accustomed to it. That's why I told you, you need a sense of humor around here," she replied.

"I guess you're right, Rose", he agreed, shrugging his shoulders at the unpleasant situation that had just transpired.

Seconds later, John entered the office and Rose made the necessary introductions.

John was a younger guy, fresh out of college. He was eager and had an extremely pleasant character. Max liked him instantly!

"So John, where are we going?" questioned Max.

"Over to the Mall to shoot some babes!" was his eager reply.

I'm lost John! Babes…what babes?" Max asked. His interest was growing by the second.

"We are supposed to be taking pictures of some celebrity divas…you know babes…divas…same thing!" exclaimed John, sounding as excited as a boy scout, off on his first camping trip.

"Actually, Whitney and Mariah are in town for a fund-raising concert to help under privileged children and they are at the Mall giving an interview. Thomas wants us to cover it. So you see Max, we're going to shoot babes!" John enthusiastically explained.

"Whatever you say, John" said Max as he followed him through the door, cameras strung over his shoulder. Max had to try desperately to keep up with John, who was behaving like a kid on his way to a candy store.,

On the way to the Mall, the two got to know each other. They engaged in conversation about a wide range of topics during the drive over, but when they arrived, the two photographers clicked into their best professional mode.

As a result the assignment went like clockwork and the photo session with the two celebrities went extremely well.

However, the day's activity seemed to end all too quickly and when they returned to the office, everyone, including Rose, gathered around. They were all eager to hear about Whitney and Mariah.

"Hey! Max how was your first assignment with John? Did you two get into any trouble?" Thomas asked, as he quickly assumed the leadership role of the inquisitive group that had formed around the two photographers.

"It was hectic, but I had a good time. Believe me, John made sure of that!" answered Max.

Then…as quickly as he had joined the group, Thomas left…always as busy as ever…off taking care of business!

As Thomas was out of sight, Rose continued with the questions, "So how were Whitney and Mariah? Do they look as good as they do on television?

More than willing to satisfy her curiosity, Max replied. "Those two are drop-dead gorgeous and they know it! I was a little surprised though. I never expected them to be so down to earth. They're very friendly."

Max continued on, "I guess you can't judge a book by its cover. You might be surprised by what's inside!"

After getting her bellyful of the two "babes" that John and Max had photographed, Rose quickly changed gears into dutiful, ever efficient secretary and broke the mode by informing Max, There's another assignment at three o'clock at the Government Building and Thomas wants you to cover it."

"What's it about? He asked.

"Some speech the Prime Minister is going to make about the state of the economy and what he intends to do to improve it." Rose explained.

"But, Rose…That is not my department! You know I only cover models and celebrities" Max protested.

"I know Max, but Thomas says he wants you to get accustomed to photographing different types of events. I guess you could discuss it with him if you like," she offered, in her sweet voice.

"No. That's ok. I will have to take what I get until I get what I want…Right, Rose?" Max replied in an attempt at regaining his composure.

"My sentiments exactly!" she agreed, before reassuring him, "Don't worry, John will go with you!"

So the days went by and each day Max was kept busy with all sorts of varying assignments. Sometimes alone. Sometimes with John.

Days quickly turned into weeks and the relationship between Rose and Max began to grow closer and closer, until one morning she approached him and said, "Can I tell you something, Max?"

"Sure. Go ahead," he told her.

"I was planning to quit my job before you arrived, but after I met you, I realized that you are different from the rest, so I decided to stay on. However, my daughter is pushing me to quit and stay at home, but I think that would drive me insane. I need to work, Max! I love to work" Rose said…a slight bit of her tightly concealed emotions beginning to show.

"So you have a daughter?" Max managed to ask in an attempt at gaining some control of the situation.

"Yes. I do…and a son too, but he lives in Europe with his wife and kids. It's sad though, because I don't get to see him very often. So, it's just Roxanne…That's my daughter's name," Rose explained.

"Good for you! As for me, Rose, I too miss my family!" Max confessed.

"So you have a family?" she asked.

"Yes. I have a wife and two adorable girls who keep me very busy and very happy" he boasted.

"I'm glad to hear that, Max! Most men these days are so busy with their careers that they forget they have a family. It's good to see that there are some of you who care about other things…other than your career." Rose replied.

"That's good to know you approve. So when am I going to meet this daughter of yours? I hope I do before I leave. I only have three months to play with," said Max

"You'll meet her…you can be sure of that!" Rose replied, in a suspiciously jovial manner.

Just then, the phone rang and Rose quickly answered it, breaking the brief bonding session with her new boss. "Thomas wants to see you in his office, a.s.a.p." she said.

"Thanks, Rose" Max shouted over his shoulder, as he bolted through the door, down the corridor, heading for Thomas' office.

CHAPTER THREE

As the weeks went by, Max became more and more proficient in his new job. Thomas' confidence in him grew to the point where he thought he could rely on him more and more.

Then, one morning Thomas invited Max to his office.

"Max...come in...make yourself comfortable. I called you to my office to talk to you about your job" Thomas said as Max entered.

"What about my job?" Max asked...all sorts of negative thoughts running through his head.

"Don't get defensive Max...relax! I was just wondering about the possibility of you staying on permanently," Thomas explained.

"Whoa...Thomas...in case you've forgotten, I have a wife and two kids back home. I promised them I would only be staying for three months. I admit that I like it here, but I have to get back to my family!" Max admitted.

"Max...you know as well as I do, you don't have to go back. Let me make a long story short...do you want the job or not? I'm sure that you can convince the little lady to either move here with you or let you stay here and she can visit with the girls as often as she likes...all expenses paid. So what do you think, Max?" Thomas asked in an almost pushy manner.

"I think she would never agree to that", was all that Max could reply.

"Well Max...I expect you to convince her. I need you just as much as you need me, Max. So you have to convince her," pleaded Thomas.

That week, Max spent hours upon hours going over in his mind how he could approach Kara on the subject of him staying in Trinidad.

Finally, the day came when he had to make the telephone call and have the conversation with her.

To his surprise, things went more smoothly than he could have ever imagined. After reiterating all of the financial benefits of him taking on the job permanently, plus the fact that it would cost them nothing, when she and the kids visited, she agreed that they would try it and see how it would work out. However, she would not commit to migrating to Trinidad right away. For now, they would see how they could cope with the visiting routine.

That day, as he spoke to Kara, Max told her how happy he was in his new job and he reassured her that she and the girls could come to see him anytime they wanted to. She was happy for him.

Borrowing some well-known lyrics, Max asked her to put her sweet lips a little closet to phone and pretend that they were together all alone.

Water almost came to his eyes when Kara said, "Honey, I love you."

Filled with emotion, Max replied, "If love was a flower sprinkled with dew, I'd pick it and send it to you. Love is so precious and not easy to part. Honey, you have all the love from my heart! Goodbye honey. I love you."

…And with that, he hung up the phone…tears streaming down both of his cheeks. It was as if a sixth sense was already forewarning him of the things to come.

Then, as if like clockwork, only days later, Roxanne, Rose's daughter, showed up at her mother's office, looking all sweet and juicy.

"Hi mom!" she said.

"Hi Roxanne! Nice to see you, girl. You're looking good," her mother replied, a proud feeling coming over her as she took in the beauty of her daughter.

"Thanks mom…but stop hugging me," gasped Roxanne from within the firm hug of her loving mother. Roxanne always felt uneasy when her mother openly displayed her affection for her, particularly in front of the people who Rose worked with.

She also didn't like the fact that her mother was always trying to set her up. Always trying to find *"Mr. Right"* for her.

Then, to no surprise to Roxanne, Rose said, "Come on… there's someone I want you to meet. His name is Max… he's a nice guy and you'll love him!"

"Here we go again!" Roxanne thought as she obediently followed Rose.

The two of them went gingerly into Max's office... mother pulling daughter by the hand---eager to do the introduction.

"Hi Max. This is my daughter, Roxanne. She teaches at one of the Primary Schools in the village not far from here. You two get to know each other, while I get some work done!" exclaimed Rose. And, as quickly as she had arrived, she left to do her tasks for the day, being the busy "worker-bee" that she was.

"I'm Roxanne," the young lady said softly. The sweetness of her voice beckoned to Max as he took in her radiance.

Then, uncontrollably, like a schoolboy out on his first prom date, Max did something childish, but yet adorable. He took Roxanne by the hand and said, while looking into her full brown eyes, "God...you're beautiful...I don't want to let go of your hand!"

Immediately, Roxanne's heart melted from this direct *"come on"* this total stranger had given her. Yet she somehow managed to say, "So what do you do around here?"

"Well…I take care of business," Max answered, copying a favorite line from his boss, Thomas.

"What kind of business?" she pressed.

"All kinds of business!" he said, deliberately being evasive.

"That's interesting," she commented, starting to get the picture that he was not going to come straight with her… at least not at that time.

"So how would you like to go on a date with me?" Max asked her.

"A date? You don't waste any time, do you?" she asked.

"The race is for the swift" be bragged.

Then and there, Max knew he had struck a good note with her, but he wasn't quite prepared for what happened next.

Roxanne walked over to his desk and raised her sexy leg on his chair and seductively said "Eight o'clock tonight, ok?"

Max couldn't believe his luck! He had been introduced to this beautiful girl, only moments earlier and already he had made a date with her. He was so excited, he couldn't concentrate. So he decided to call it quits for the day and head home.

"She sure had delicious looking lips," he couldn't help thinking on his way home.

She too, was thinking about him. He had the sexiest eyes and was dark and handsome too. She didn't know a thing about him or his past. She simply just wanted a piece of his body! She was out of control with lust! *"Thanks, mummy!"* she thought, *"You've finally given me something I could work with!"*

And…with that, Roxanne too hurried home. She couldn't wait to share the good news of her new *"find"* with one of her close friends. So as she got through her apartment door, she was on the phone to her very best friend, Liz.

Liz was an undercover cop. Liz was also a very talented exotic dancer. She was just great in whatever she did…be it an undercover cop or a dance.

When Liz answered the phone, Roxanne exclaimed, "Girl I am going out with this great guy tonight and if I tell you he is great, he is!"

"He must be some kind of guy," Liz replied, feeling happy for her friend.

"Liz…Trust me. It seems that today was the greatest day of my life!" Roxanne confided.

On Max's way home, he stopped at a store and picked up some sexy underwear and had it wrapped and delivered to Roxanne's. He had gotten the address from her mother, earlier at work.

When she received the lingerie, Roxanne immediately fell in love with it and put it on, in anticipation of a hot evening to come. She thought that he really knew how to take are of business!

Shortly afterwards, Max rang her doorbell and when she opened the door, she looked like the angel of his dreams. Even though he wanted her there and then, Max stuck to his plan and they drove off to the finest restaurant in town, with him ensuring to be the perfect gentleman, opening the car door for her and escorting her in a fashion that befitted royalty.

In her mind, Roxanne must have known it was going to be a good night!

At the restaurant, the light was low. The music was right and the drinks started to flow. Roxanne started to give Max signs that she wanted his body close to hers, but tried to retain her ladylike composure as she looked into his eyes and spurted out. "Max, I like you more than you can imagine!"

"Is that so?" he asked.

"Yes! She assured him, "What do you think about that?"

"I think you've had too much to drink. Let's take a walk on the beach. After all, it's our first date. We both have a lot to learn about each other," he told her.

"You're so right, Max!" she admitted.

So they walked along the beach holding hands and making small talk with each other. Afterwards, they returned to the restaurant and danced the night away to Otis Redding, holding each other tenderly. It is then and there that they both decided that they would be together as an item.

CHAPTER FOUR

The next day, Max was at work early when Thomas called him to his office.

"Max…it's over a month since you're here and I feel comfortable knowing that you can handle the business. So I'm going off island for two days…and guess what… you're in charge," he explained.

Without giving Max a chance to respond, he went on to say, "I heard that you like Roxanne."

Max felt like he had committed a crime, when Thomas said that. He knew it was just a matter of time before everyone learnt the truth about his feeling towards Roxanne, but he could not bring himself to admit it just yet. So he replied, "I don't want to hurt her feelings. For now she's just a friend. I have to be careful not to get too much involved."

Inside Max told himself that he didn't want to be a heart breaker, but it did seem to him that somebody was going to get hurt. He loved his wife very much, but he knew that one night with Roxanne had changed his life. They hadn't made love, but the time they spent together was just great!

Max left Thomas with that half-truth of an explanation and returned to his office, where Rose was busy as usual, checking on assignment schedules and making appointments.

"Hi Rose. Any messages for me?" He asked.

"Oh, yes. Your wife called and don't forget the meeting with the guy from the nightclub at 11:30 a.m." she replied.

"Thanks, Rose," he said. He knew she wanted to ask him about the night before by the way she was looking at him.

"Is everything ok, Rose?" he asked.

"Well yes…but, by the way…are you free for lunch tomorrow? There is something I wanted to talk to you about," Rose replied.

Max felt so ashamed when she said, "Not to worry, it isn't about Roxanne." He was relieved, but knew that Roxanne's name would have to come up before long.

Just then, the phone rang, and Rose picked it up. "Hello. Hi. How are you doing?" Max heard her say. Then she said, "Hold on…Max, it's for you," as she handed him the phone and trotted through the door.

"Don't forget lunch tomorrow. Let's say around 2:00 p.m." Max shouted after her.

Moments later, after had had finished his brief telephone conversation, Max went down the corridor to take a drink at the water cooler. He was only gone a few minutes, but when he returned…there was Roxanne!

She was sitting on his desk; her legs folded in a suggestive manner; her pretty smile was ever so inviting.

Max thought, *"T&T is a much faster place than where I came from"*. In fact…it was looking like it was too fast for him!

However, he was already strapped into high gear. There was no turning back!

So, he and Roxanne saw each other as often as they could during the course of the week and they made plans to get together at his apartment on the weekend.

The rendezvous was set for Friday at 8:00 p.m.

When Friday evening came, Max got busy with the preparations. He set the table and asked himself what was next? Max knew he wanted to give a good impression. He desperately wanted to set the mood, so he put in a red bulb in the ceiling to set the atmosphere. It was really romantic.

He lit some candles and put them in his flowerpot so that the light between the plant and the roof beamed between the pot and ceiling. Next, he put on soft music in the background and changed into his best designer outfit. The dinner was ready and so was he.

At eight, Rosanne arrived on queue…dressed to kill!

They had a lovely dinner, engaging in deep conversation. After they finished eating, they began to dance – her hand moving up and down his spine, turning him on tremendously.

Max started to nibble on her ear and slowly his tongue found its way to the tip of her nose. He knew she was enjoying it by the way she was pressing her head against his shoulder.

Roxanne put her lips against Max's chest and opened his shirt with her teeth and quickly moved her tongue across his chest like a hot knife gliding through butter.

"Max, can we shower?" she whispered...and before she could say anything else, both of their clothes were off.

He lifted her nude body into the bath and together they explored every crevice of each other's body, as the water cascaded down the curves of their sexuality. Max almost took her all the way in the shower, but he somehow managed to remain in control. He lifted her once more and took her to his bed.

She waited impatiently as he climbed on top of her soft body, her warm sensitive core wanting him the worst possible way. Then and there, they both lost total control. She grabbed his head and pressed their lips together as he entered her warmth.

"I love you, Max!" she whispered, "You are the only man I will ever need."

Before he could respond, she asked, "Do you love me, Max? Be careful…if you say you love me, make sure its from your heart!"

Max was lost for words…not wanting to admit to the intense feelings he had for her!

Roxanne was having the time of her life. She really enjoyed the passionate sex they had together. She felt so comfortable with Max.

She had told her mother that she was going out with Max and Rose hadn't seemed to mind. All Rose had told her was that he was a nice guy.

Roxanne was convinced that Max was now a major part of her life. He was simply too good to let go!

CHAPTER FIVE

During the course of the following week, Roxanne's girl-friend, Liz was working under cover at a popular nightclub in the area. Her superior had briefed her to keep an eye on a particular shady group of characters that frequented the club. They were suspected drug dealers.

This was the perfect assignment because it jelled well with her second past time as an exotic dancer.

However, not all of her assignments were this appealing to her! She was sometimes placed in very precarious situations where her life was at stake.

Sometimes she felt like quitting, but she had a daughter whose father was not supporting her, so she needed the money.

Her six-year old daughter didn't know exactly what she did for a living. She knew Liz was a Police Officer, but that was all. The undercover bit was kept a secret from her.

Liz loved her daughter very much. If only she had a father to hug and give her his love, it would have been so nice, Liz thought. Yet she knew that someday a good man would come around and be there for her.

Then, on Wednesday night, it seemed that her prayers were answered. It was like a dream come through.

She was on stage dancing when two guys came in and sat at the bar. They ordered two drinks. Her eyes were on one instantly.

They were also looking at her. She was in the midst of her strip routine when the DJ changed the music to a more seductive beat, causing her to really go to work! She couldn't control herself. She simply let herself go. She wanted this man to notice her above all the other dancers in the club. She didn't know why. She just wanted his attention!

After the dance routine was finished, she walked over to the men and asked the one who she fancied, "Who are you looking at?" with a voice that would have turned an angry beast into a helpless lamb.

He looked at her and smiled, "Who do you think I'm looking at, sugar?"

Liz knew from the time that she looked into his face and he opened his mouth that he was hers. She took his glass and sipped from it, while rubbing her curvy body close to him.

"Like what you see?" she whispered.

"What can I say? You have a great body!" he replied.

"Thanks, What you see is what you get." Liz purred.

"How would I know? I never bought a car, unless I test-drove it. So if you are as good as you look, I'll like to prove it," the man eagerly replied.

Liz knew that this guy was hers for the taking. She could feel it. She sat on his leg, moved her finger across his chest very slowly and breathed in his face. Then she said, "I will give you the ride of your life...you will never forget"

I'm...I'm...I'm looking...looking forward to it" he stammered. His voice was barely audible.

Liz held his hand, took out a pen and wrote her number in his palm. "Call me. I will be waiting," she said, as she walked to the door. She stopped just before the exit and looked around. The man blew a kiss at her and, in response, Liz moved her tongue over her lips, as if she had tasted something sweet.

Everything was in place. All she was waiting on was that call!

And…as luck would have it, a few evenings later, Liz's mother visited her and asked if her grand daughter could spend the night with her.

"Sure! No problem," Liz replied. She loved her daughter, but sometimes she cherished a little solitude. It was good for the soul.

After her mother and daughter left, Liz grabbed a book she was meaning to finish reading for quit a while and nestled into her favorite chair.

She was just getting into the story, when, about 7:30 p.m., the phone rang.

"Hello, I am hearing sounds like gunshots outside my door. Could you come and check it out for me?" The person on the other end of the line asked.

Liz knew the male voice on the other end of the line immediately. It was the man who she had flirted with only nights before at the club.

He gave her his address and she quickly wrote it down on a piece of paper. It was about three miles away, so she jumped into her car and sped to meet him.

When she arrived at the address, Liz leaned on the doorbell and he opened the door. She was tempted to ask him about the gunshots, but she knew that he had made up that story. She knew that the so-called *"gun shots"* were merely an attempt by him to break the ice with her.

However, she wondered how he knew that she was an undercover cop. By all rights, he should have just thought that she was simply a dancer who worked at the club. What she didn't know was that Thomas knew the owner of the club and in a conversation with him, Thomas learnt that he was cooperating with the police in some sort of undercover operation.

Having learnt all the details, Thomas, in one of his many confidential conversations with his new, trusted employee filled Max in.

Liz was taken in by the view she got of his body. She noticed that he was not wearing anything, but a skimpy brief.

He smiled and said, "My…You're looking good! Come on in. As you can see I am wet. I am working out. I hope I am not wasting your time.

Mesmerized by the sight of his near nakedness, Liz went inside, eager to find out where this encounter was heading.

"Let me show you where I am working out," he said again, without giving Liz a chance to reply.

As he turned his body, Liz got a good look at his firmness as he led her down to his workout room.

Her mouth was watering just by looking at his almost nude body. The window was open as a soft breeze blew in, making her nipples tense with anxiety.

"You know, I can arrest you for a false alarm," she said in a soft voice, referring to his *"made-up"* story about the gunshots.

However, she was standing too close to him and when he took another step, her whole body pressed against his raw flesh. He smiled…the bulge in the front of his shorts seemed to coil and uncoil against the front of Liz's thigh-fitted skirt, like a snake trying to attach. Seconds later, she was running her hands up and down his muscular body.

The man bent down and kissed Liz. The inside of his mouth was sweet, as if he had just swallowed a glass of wine. As he put his strong arms around her, she became moist. Something like that had never happened to her before!

She was like magic in his hands. She wanted to feel him inside of her, but her conscience told her it was too soon to take this any further.

I'm sorry. Can we just talk?" she said.

"No…I'm sorry I came on to you like that," he replied.

"That's ok. I needed it," Liz confessed.

"What?" he said, seeking an explanation.

"I meant it has been a long time I have not been with a man. Let me take it from the top. I need some good loving, but I'm not a whore," she explained.

He was beginning to get the picture, so he replied in a gentle voice, saying "Come, sit down and relax. I will get you something to drink."

With that, he got two glasses of wine and said, "Let's start over…By the way, Liz…my name's Max. I found out your name from the owner of the club. He told me you were working undercover and I just had to meet you."

The man of her dreams…Max, whom she had met only nights ago at the nightclub, smiled and she put her hands around him and kissed his face, while leaning her head on him.

"This is nice," she thought. Secretly she wondered if her daughter was going to like him.

CHAPTER SIX

The following day Roxanne was in her classroom teacher her students to count to ten. The children began to recite the numbers out loud, but stopped at five abruptly.

Puzzled, Roxanne looked around at the doorway to see what had caused the children to lose their concentration. And…there standing at the door was Max!

She smiled…Her day could not have been better! "Oh my God!" she thought, "He looked so good standing there!"

"Excuse me class," she said, as she walked to the door. "Hi, Max. This is a surprise!" she blurted, "I'm glad to see you here!"

Quickly thinking on her next move, she asked him to watch her class for two minutes, while she went to the ladies room. It was just a cover so that she could catch her breath and clear her head. The sight of this man standing there at the doorway of the classroom simply made her dizzy with desire. She felt so good that she almost started to cry. This man certainly had an effect on her, she thought. Only, she couldn't begin to understand why. After all, they had only been together twice and had made love only once.

When Roxanne returned to the class, Max and the children were having a good time together. Max seemed to be having fun and the children seemed to attach themselves to him, as if by magic. *"How does he do that? What makes him so special?"* she wondered to herself. *"Anyway, once he's with me…that's all that matters!"*

It was just about break time, so Roxanne sent the children out into the playground, so she could have Max all to herself. She held his hand and pulled it to her aching body.

He put his arms around her and squeezed her tight… just like the night on the beach. Roxanne felt just like a princess in a fairytale as she leaned back in his arms with one leg held high behind her, allowing a feeling of ecstasy to engulf her.

After the moment was over, she straightened up herself and told Max, "Baby…thanks for dropping by. You've made my day…it's time for the children to come back in though…I'll call you when I get home later."

As he was leaving, Max turned around, blew her a kiss and said, "Bye for now, Rox…Be good!"

Later that afternoon, Roxanne called her girlfriend Liz and asked if she could meet her after work, so that they could go shopping…she wanted to get something new to look good for her man, Max!

"Sure! I'll meet you at the Mall at 4:00 p.m." Liz answered… feeling all excited. This was an opportunity to tell her friend Roxanne about the new flame in her life!

While shopping, Roxanne began to tell Liz about her new boyfriend, Max.

"Max!" exclaimed Liz.

"Do you know him?" asked Roxanne.

Liz thought for a moment and then decided…no…it couldn't be…This must just be a coincidence! After all, there might be hundreds of men in T&T named Max!

"No, Rox…Just the name sounds familiar," she finally answered.

"I don't think you know him…He's new in town. He works with my mother," Roxanne replied, wondering about the puzzled look on her friend's face, "Liz! Are you all right?"

Liz thought for a while. "Oh yes. I'm all right!" she answered. Then quickly changing the subject, she said, "Look at this dress and there are the shoes to match it! I'm going to the bathroom. I'll be back shortly."

In the bathroom, Liz put two and two together and came to the conclusion that she and her best fried, Roxanne, were in fact, dating the same man! To her sharp police-trained mind, the evidence was clear. There was only one "Max" working at the advertising agency where Roxanne's mother worked!

Liz thought out loud, "God! She's my best friend, but I can't let her take this man of my dreams! I'm not going to tell her, nor am I going to confront Max about her! That'll ruin everything and I can't afford to let him walk away. I'm sorry, Roxanne. We have to compete and may the best woman win! I promise that the next time Max and I meet; I'm going all the way. I just need to know what he likes and how he likes it! This time, I'll do the inviting… to my place."

Then an idea struck her. She would let Roxanne provide her with all of the kinky details that she would need to please her man. After all, it was her job as an undercover cop to dig up clues in a secretive and sometimes devious manner!

Eventually, Liz went back to where Roxanne was waiting and helped her to choose an outfit from the store.

The two friends spent the better part of the three hours at the mall, during which, Liz got Roxanne to give her all that she needed to know about Max. It was easy; Roxanne just couldn't help bragging to her best friend about the new lover.

The next morning, Roxanne went to work. To her surprise, the children were all waiting for her to arrive. This was something they never did!

"Good morning children," she addressed them.

"Good morning teacher," they answered in unison.

"My, you bunch are early today. What's the occasion?" she questioned.

Roxanne was shocked when the entire class, all at once, shouted, "Because we want to see your boyfriend again. We like him and we want him to visit us again! Are you going to marry him, teacher?"

Roxanne had to quickly sit down in her chair in order not to trip over. Her legs were trembling and her stomach was churning. She knew marriage was out of the question. After all, Max was married…but could it be that her feelings for Max were that obvious? Even these young children could read her like a book.

It took her a while, but in an effort to retain control, she brought herself to say, "You know, if you promise not to ask me any more questions like this, I will take you out on a field trip on Saturday and maybe, just maybe…he'll come with us!"

The next day, the children were busy writing an exam. Roxanne was watching on, ensuring that the little ones did not get into any mischief. She knew that, given a chance, some of them would be tempted to cheat.

She began to daydream about Max, but was interrupted by her co-worker, Jeff, who popped his head inside the classroom door.

"Hi Roxanne," he said.

"Hi Jeff," she replied; a bit annoyed that he had broken her train of though about her man.

"Can I buy you lunch today?" Jeff continued. He had a thing for her and he thought he would make his move.

Knowing just where Jeff was leading, Roxanne asked him, "What's on your mind Jeff?"

"I was thinking that maybe we could be good friends," he confessed.

"Get lost Jeff!" she exclaimed…putting him in his place. She was head over heels in love with Max and did not have any time for any other man.

"I am serious," he offered, simply refusing to accept rejection.

"Me too, Jeff!" she replied. "The only way we'll be together is if we were swallowed by the same fish!"

"You'll need me someday, Roxanne!" he told her sarcastically.

"Not even in your dreams!" she teased.

He was mad, but she didn't give a damn. Reluctantly, Jeff left. His face was pouting. His feelings hurt. Roxanne couldn't care less!

She let her thoughts drift back to her man, Max. *"What is Max doing at work?"* she wondered, *"I think that I should give him a call."*

She picked up the phone, but changed her mind. She would see him later. *"One touch from him and I would be as good as gold!"* she said to herself.

Noon was near and the children finished writing their exam.

"Class, its time for lunch," she informed them. "Enjoy your lunch children...ok?"

"Yes teacher!" they replied. They all loved her. She was their favorite teacher. She was like a second mother to most of them.

CHAPTER SEVEN

Liz called Max. He was not at home, so she left a message for him, asking him to call her when he got home.

She then jumped into her car and rushed to the mall to buy the sexiest lingerie she could find.

She knew she had to look good for her man!

Max retrieved her message at about 7:00 p.m. He immediately called her and said he would be at her place at 8:45 p.m.

It was like a dream come true for Liz. She wanted to do something very hot and wild for Max! she had to convince him that she was the one for him.

She went over her plans for the evening. She would make sure that he would spend the whole night with her.

Liz put a bottle of wine to chill and, once she had straightened up her apartment, she sat and waited for Max to arrive.

At 8:45 p.m. precisely, Max rang Liz's doorbell.

"*Oh my God*! He is here," Liz told herself, as she rushed to open the door.

As soon as he saw her, Max took her into his arms, bent over and kissed gently on the lips.

"Good nigh, baby," he said.

"Please come in. I've been waiting for you, Max…my love. Have a seat." She replied.

She wanted to treat him like he was the "*King of the Caribbean*". She poured them each a glass of wine. "Cheers! She said, "To us!"

Secretly she thought that when she was finished with him, she would be the last woman he would ever need for the rest of his life.

A few minutes passed and Liz asked Max if he would like her to dance for him. He said, "Yes!" So she excused herself and went to slip into the lingerie she had bought earlier.

Slowly, she started to dance to a popular dancehall song that was playing on her stereo. Next, she sat on his lap and started to give him a lap dance, gyrating her hips and pelvis in a viscously seductive fashion.

Max became aroused instantly. His strong hands were soon on her hips. His body began to match hers, grind for grind.

Liz heard Max groaning and when she thought that he was losing control; she stopped dancing and asked him to go into the shower with her.

She took off his clothes and they showered together. It was great! She did everything in her power to make him happy and he asked her to tell him what turned her on the most sexually.

She couldn't stop herself from telling him all about her sexual fantasies. She told him she especially like the sixty-nine position and that she also liked to get on top of him and ride his shaft, before he flipped her over and took her from behind, doggie-style. All of this talk about sex made her wet for her man!

Liz then asked Max if he enjoyed playing out fantasies, but instead of replying, he simply swooped down, picked up her silky body, carried her to the bedroom and laid her on the bed.

Her body ached for his touch. The weight of his sexy body heated up her warm, sensitive core with the quickness. Good! She wanted him in the worst way. She was out of control, going crazy with passion.

"I love you, Max," she whispered softly into his ear. He grabbed her back and plunged his tongue into her hungry mouth. Then, in one spontaneous move, he entered her.

Their lovemaking was incredible! It was simply the best sex, Liz has ever had! She let herself go in wild abandonment, her body shaking with multiple orgasms. God! This man was simply the best!

When they were done, it felt like their bodies were joined as one. Their body chemistry gelled and Liz knew that Max was hers! She would see to that!

The following day, Roxanne phoned Max to inform him about a concert that her school was having that evening.

"Max I would love to have you there, even if it's just for a few minutes. I know you have a busy schedule, but your presence would make me feel so good. Please Max, I want you to be there," she begged.

Max, replied, "Baby, baby, hello? Can I say something now?" he interrupted.

"Sorry, honey. I just got a little carried away," she said.

"Girl, you don't know how much you mean to me. I like the kids in your class and they seem to like me too. So I wouldn't let you or them down. You can bet your life, baby, I will be there!" he assured her, before hanging up the phone.

As soon as Max got off the phone, Liz called. "Hello lover boy, I've been trying to reach you for the past half hour," Liz complained.

"As you know I am a business man, baby. I'm always on the go. So what's on your mind, honey?" he asked.

"Well, as you know, today is my day off and I have something planned for us later on and I won't take no for an answer," explained Liz.

"Is that so? I have a little something planned myself, but I can make a little adjustment. So what time are you talking about," he replied.

"About six o'clock. Is that too late for you lover boy?" she queried.

"I can work with that, my sweet chocolate," Max assured her.

"You pick me up at home around 6:00 p.m. How does that sound?" Liz asked.

Max was quick to reply, "Great! See you later then, bye! Already he was scheming about how he would manage being in two places that evening. The timing was tight, but he knew he could do it.

Roxanne's concert started at 5:00 p.m. as scheduled. Max showed up as promised, at about 5:20 p.m., just in time to listen to Roxanne's speech. He looked at her on the stage, waved his hand and she nodded her head and smiled. Feeling reassured by seeing her man come out to support her; she then headed towards the podium with a smile that would have lit up the darkest night.

Roxanne then began the opening remarks for the concert. "Good evening ladies and gentlemen, distinguished guests, boys and girls. I would like to thank each and every one of you for coming to this fund raising activity. We all know that the children will become the men and women of tomorrow and as parents, adults, teachers and guardians, it is our responsibility to raise and nourish these children and prepare them for a better tomorrow. So I am asking you to give generously for this worthy cause…"

She didn't even finish her speech when Max slipped back through the crowd and slithered through the doorway, off to his next mission for the evening.

After she had completed her introduction, Roxanne looked for Max, but he was nowhere to be found. *"He must be very busy tonight. That man of mine is all about business! Still, he took the time to come out to hear me!"* she thought. A sense of pride began to sweep through her soul.

It was around 6:30 p.m. when Max drove up to Liz's house and blew his car horn to announce his arrival. "Liz, come on out," he yelled.

"You are late!" Liz shouted back, as she ran towards the door to meet her man!

"You know what I say girl, it's better late than never," he replied, trying to impress her.

"Let's go to the beach to watch the sun set. Then we can go to my favorite bar; it's only two blocks away from here. Maybe we could have a few drinks and eat something. So how does that sound?" Liz told him, all in the same breath. She just wanted to be with him.

She would have done anything. Gone anywhere. Just as long as it was with him!

"I have a better idea, Max. Let's skip the bar and go to your apartment. I have something special in mind for you tonight!" Liz whispered.

"I always give the ladies what they want," Max replied as he turned his car towards the direction of his home and stepped on the accelerator. The woman wanted him and he was going to make sure she got what she wanted.

During the time that it took Max to reach his apartment, his phone was ringing off the hook. Roxanne was trying to get through, but no one was answering. *"He must be very busy,"* she thought. *"Maybe I'll stop by later to give him a massage to help him relax."*

Liz and Max finally arrived at his apartment. "I feel like celebrating," he told her, as he proceeded to fix them both a drink from his bar.

"And what are we celebrating, Max?" Liz asked.

"Oh…nothing except our love, baby," he replied, as smooth as ever.

Then he turned on the stereo and, as if he had personally planned it, a love song started to play, helping to set the mood.

The song did the trick. "Do you want to dance?" Liz asked, as she slipped behind him and hugged her man tightly.

"It seems as though you were reading my mind, baby" he replied.

After the song finished playing, Liz went to the bathroom to freshen up. Max went on the verandah looking at the moonlight. *"Damn"* he thought, *"tonight might be full moon."*

While he was there gazing at the moon, Liz quietly walked back into the living room and took the receiver off of the telephone. *"There would be no interruptions tonight, lover!"* she thought to herself. Then she moved seductively towards the verandah and sneaked up behind Max, put her hands around his waist and kissed the back of his neck.

"That feels good Liz. There is a question I've been wanting to ask you…do you have a degree in lovemaking?"

"Why do you ask, Max?" she replied.

"Nothing baby…it's just the way you make me feel. No one can compete. You make me feel like no other woman could…but…enough said, lets go inside."

Already feeling excited, Liz led him to the bedroom and before they knew it, they were both completely naked.

CHAPTER EIGHT

After the school concert, Roxanne decided to make good on her plan and go to Max's house. However, during the drive over, something in the back of her mind began to nag at her. She couldn't help but think that something was wrong.

"Sure Max is a busy man," she thought, *"but why couldn't he have arranged his day to spend more time at the concert. After all, he should have been delighted to see me and my students perform!"*

Maybe, something was wrong, but Roxanne loved the man and was still waiting to give him the benefit of the doubt. So, as she parked into Max's driveway, she thought, *"My man must have a legitimate explanation!"*

She tried the lock on the front door. To her delight, it was unlocked. "Great!" she said out loud. "I'll surprise my baby and sneak in to bed with him. It'll be so nice just to cuddle against my Max!"

Roxanne tiptoed through the living room. *"That's strange!"* she thought as she bent over and replaced the receiver on the phone. *"Why would the phone be off the hook?"*

Nevertheless, she wanted to focus on one thing and one thing only. Nothing could divert her thoughts now! She wanted to feel, smell and touch her man! So, she wiped all thoughts about the phone out her mind and headed straight towards her lover's bedroom.

As she approached, she had another pleasant surprise; that the door was wide open. *"So far, so good!"* she thought. *"I can't wait to get next to my man!"*

However, Roxanne's pleasant surprise swiftly turned into a full-blown, dreadful shock!

It was the kind of shock that clenched at her very soul s the reality of what she saw began to pierce her heart and crush her very existence.

There, lying fast asleep, as naked as new born babies in their birthday suits, was her best friend, Liz and her man, Max; both locked into each others arms. Every sign that the setting was the aftermath of a hot and lurid session of sex filled the air and every pour of the room.

Breath-taken, Roxanne braced herself against the jam of the bedroom door to keep from losing her ground. Her feet so weak, they could not support her.

After a few moments passed, she slowly began to regain her composure. Wiping the tears from her swollen eyes, she looked around the living room for a pen and paper to write a note.

Although, she wanted to scream at them both, Roxanne knew that she didn't have the guts to face the sleeping lovebirds. She would simply write Max to let him know that she was there, but also, and more importantly, he would know that she had witnessed the unforgivable; she had seen him in bed with her best friend!

Roxanne's note simply read, "Max, I was here, but you were fast asleep and I didn't bother to wake you. Roxanne." She then placed it on the clipboard on his refrigerator and left the apartment, another stream of tears flowing down her cheeks.

The next morning, Liz was already awake in the kitchen making her man's breakfast when the phone rang. She was somewhat puzzled because she knew she had taken it off the hook the night before and she didn't recall Max getting out of bed, much less, replacing the receiver back on the hook.

While that thought was going through her head, the phone rang once again and Max ran out of the bedroom to answer it.

"Hello Max. It's Roxanne," the voice on the other end said.

"Hi baby how are you doing?" Max whispered, not wanting Liz to hear.

"Oh, I'm ok…did you go to the fridge for the morning?" Roxanne replied.

Puzzled, Max asked, "No! Why do you ask?"

"I left something for you on the fridge door. Just check it out. I have to go now" was the reply that he received, just prior to a loud "*click*" as Roxanne hung up.

A cold sweat began to engulf Max's body as he started to realize that Roxanne was up to something! "*What's she done? Has she found out about Liz and I? Does Liz know about Roxanne?*" he asked himself.

His worst fears turned into harsh reality when he hung up the phone and turned around to face Liz standing behind him with Roxanne's note in her hand!

Max started to open his mouth in an attempt to offer an explanation, but, to his surprise, Liz stopped him by placing her fingers over his mouth. Instead of giving him the cursing of his life that he was expecting, she smiled and embraced him tightly. Her body still felt warm and cozy from the heated session the night before.

It was then that Max realized that Liz had known about Roxanne all along. She had known, but didn't care because she knew what she wanted and did what it took to get it. He realized that in the world of *"Players"* he was a mere *"Jack of Spades"*, while Liz was a *"Queen of Hearts"*.

Smiling to himself, he began to fondle Liz all over, making her hot and horny. As they sank to the floor, right there in the middle of his living room, he couldn't help thinking that he still had a few aces up his sleeve.

The women in T&T, that he had met, brought out a side of him that he had not known existed and there was no turning back now.

Even as he entered Liz, Max was already thinking about his next "*mission*" to conquer what his new environment had to offer in the way of the opposite sex.

Later that night, after he had dropped Liz off at her home, Max dropped by the same nightclub where he had first met her. He went directly to the bar and ordered a stiff drink, all the while, planning his next caper.

Then, out of the corner of his eye, he glanced at an attractive young lady, sitting a couple of stools away from him. She was slowly sipping on her drink, swirling a straw between her lips. "*Oh yeah*," he thought, "*Bingo*!"

Jumping into gear, Max eased his way toward her and sat down on the stool next to her.

"Hi...I'm Max and you are?" he said.

"What do you want?" the young lady asked.

"Come on girl. Don't be like that. Take it easy. I may not be the one of your dreams or, for that matter, the most handsome man you've seen, but if you would just give me a chance to prove myself to you, I guarantee you will never forget it," Max replied in the best "*come on*" tone of voice.

"If I give you a chance, what will that do for me?" the young lady replied, somewhat intrigued with the boldness of this man whom she had never met before in her life.

She had bitten the bait. Max was in luck. He quickly said "I will make you the happiest woman on earth. I'll satisfy your every need."

With that, the young lady smiled. She produced a card from her purse with her name and telephone number and bent over to slip it into Max's shirt pocket. Max could feel her warm breath tickle his neck, but before he could react, the young lady got up and disappeared through the crown that had begun to gather in the club.

What would be the outcome of this tangled web of lust and desire? Will Max resolve things with Roxanne? Will Liz remain with him? Will Max hit it off with this new mystery lady? These and more questions will be answered in the next book…"**TWINS IN LOVE" DOUBLE THE PLEASURE!"**

The End